The Nature Garden

written by Jay Dale
photography by Ned Meldrum

At school we have a nature garden.
We have lots of plants and animals.

Here is our teacher.
She always helps us in the garden.
She helps us with the animals, too.

In the garden we have lots of *vegetables*.

In the garden we have *peas*, *tomatoes* and *carrots*. We have *lettuce*, too.

We can put the vegetables in a *salad*.
We sit at the *picnic tables* to eat the salad.

In the classroom we have lots of animals.

We always look after them.

We have *lizards*, *guinea pigs* and a *rabbit*.

We have a pet *snake*, too.

The rabbits and guinea pigs like to eat carrots from the garden.

The snake is brown and white.
It lives in a big *glass cage*.
We can take the snake
out of the cage.
We are not scared of it!

On hot days, we eat lunch by the *pond*.

We look at the little animals that live in the pond, too.

We have lots of *chickens* at school.
Some are black and some are brown.
They give us *eggs*.
The chickens live in a chicken house.

We all **love** the nature garden.

Picture Glossary

 carrots

 guinea pigs

 picnic tables

 tomatoes

 chickens

 lettuce

 rabbit

 vegetables

 eggs

 lizards

 salad

 pond

 glass cage

 peas

 snake